COLDPLAY
FOR UKULELE

ISBN 978-1-4584-9434-4

HAL•LEONARD®
CORPORATION
7777 W. BLUEMOUND RD. P.O. BOX 13819 MILWAUKEE, WI 53213

Visit Hal Leonard Online at
www.halleonard.com

CONTENTS

Brothers and Sisters

Words and Music by Guy Berryman, Jon Buckland, Will Champion and Chris Martin

Additional Lyrics

2. Brothers and sisters feel fine.
   It's the time of your lives.
   It's the time of your lives.
   There's no sound, no sound
   Like this feeling you've found,
   Like this feeling you've found.

Clocks

Words and Music by Guy Berryman, Jon Buckland, Will Champion and Chris Martin

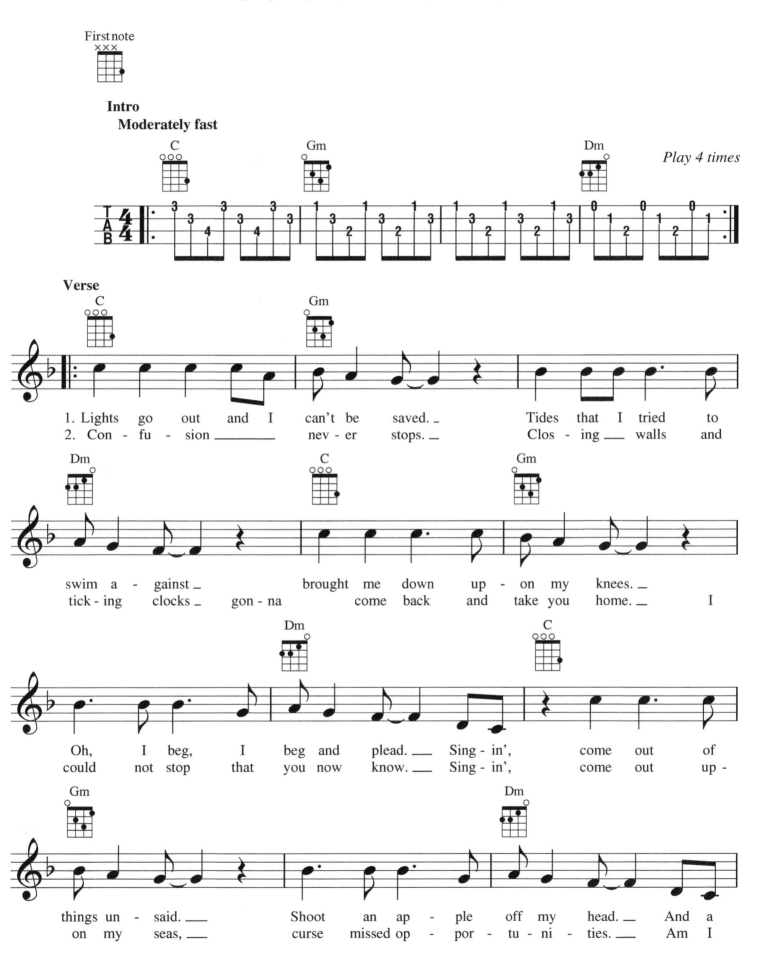

trou - ble that can't be named. ___ A ti - ger's wait - ing to be tamed. ___ } Sing-in', ___
a part ___ of the cure ___ or am I part of the dis - ease? ___ }

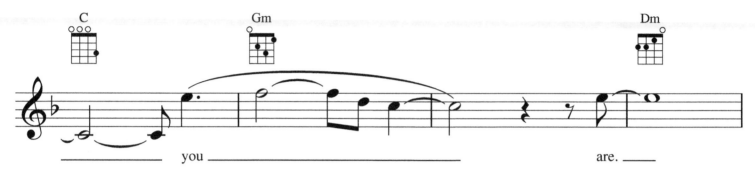

_____ you _____ are. ____

You _____ are. ____

1. Interlude

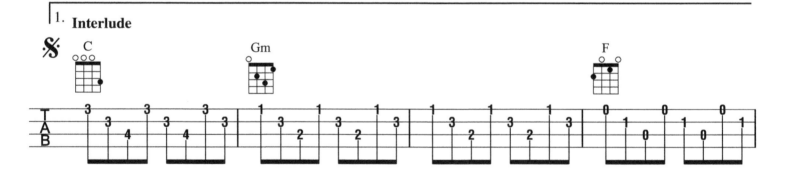

To Coda

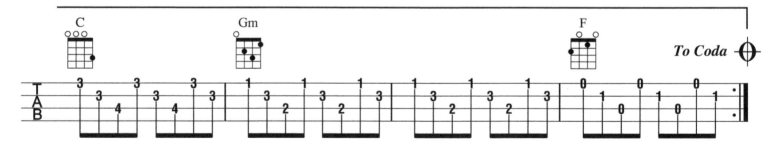

2.

You _____ are. ____

Every Teardrop Is a Waterfall

Words and Music by Guy Berryman, Jon Buckland, Will Champion, Chris Martin,
Peter Allen, Adrienne Anderson and Brian Eno

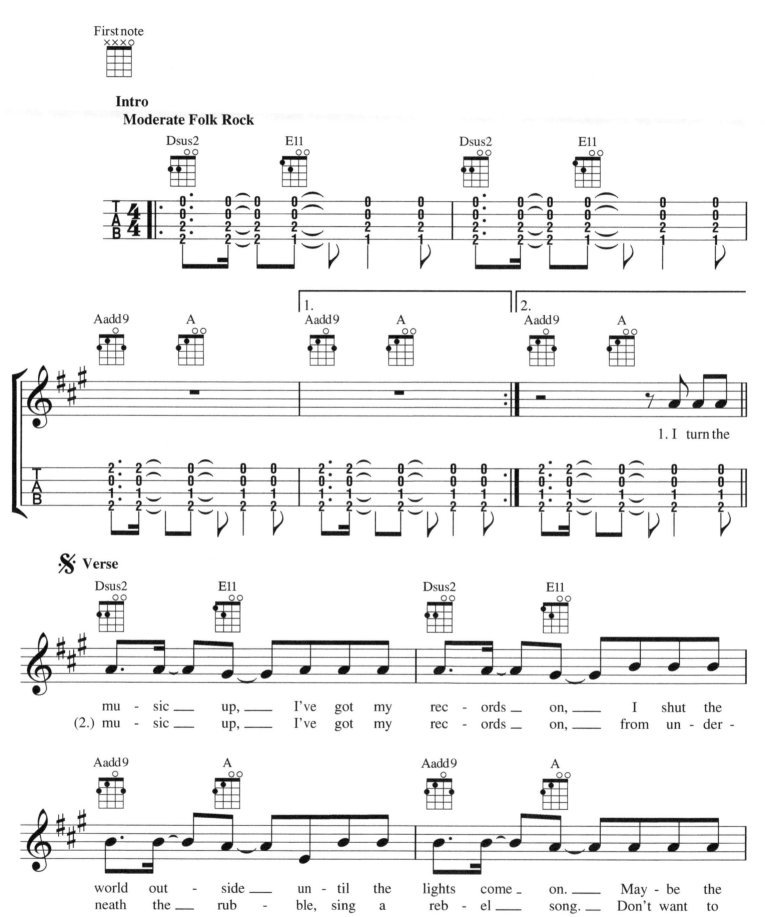

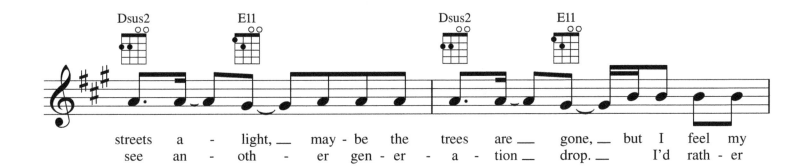

streets a - light, __ may - be the trees are __ gone, __ but I feel my
see an - oth - er gen - er - a - tion __ drop. __ I'd rath - er

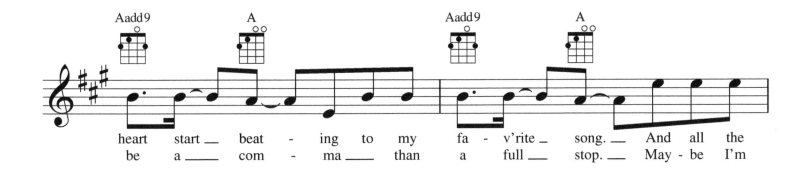

heart start __ beat - ing to my fa - v'rite __ song. __ And all the
be a __ com - ma __ than a full __ stop. __ May - be I'm

kids, they __ dance, __ all the kids, all __ night, __ un - til
in the __ black, __ may - be I'm on my __ knees, __ may - be I'm

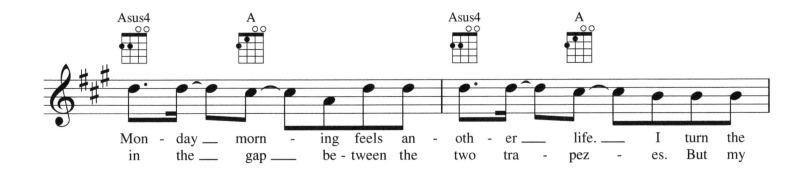

Mon - day __ morn - ing feels an - oth - er __ life. __ I turn the
in the __ gap __ be - tween the two tra - pez - es. But my

To Coda ⊕

mu - sic __ up, __ I'm on a roll this __ time, __ and
heart is __ beat - ing and my puls - es __ start __ ca -

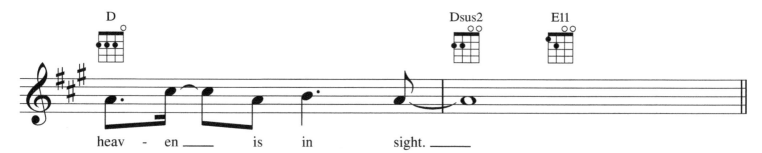

heav - en ____ is in sight. ____

Interlude

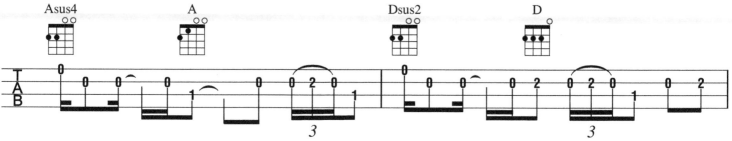

D.S. al Coda

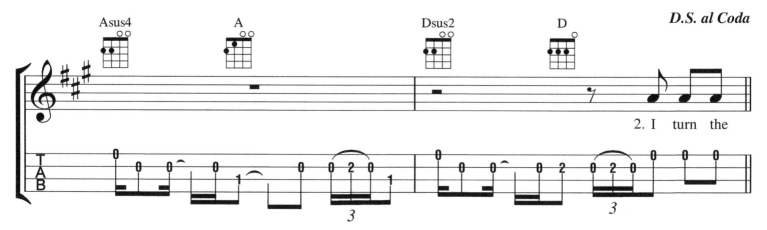

2. I turn the

the - drals ___ in my heart. ____ As we ____

Bridge

saw, whoa, _____ this ___ light, ____

I swear you e - merge blink - ing ___ in - to, to

tell me ___ it's al - right. ___ As we ___ soar walls, ___

___ ev-'ry si-ren is a sym - pho-ny. ___ And ev - 'ry tear's a

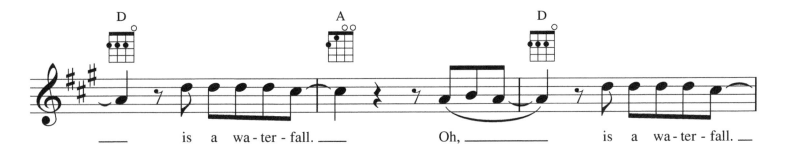

wa - ter - fall, ___ is a wa-ter-fall. ___ Oh, ___

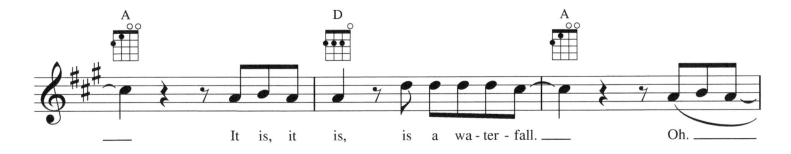

___ is a wa-ter-fall. ___ Oh, ___ is a wa-ter-fall. ___

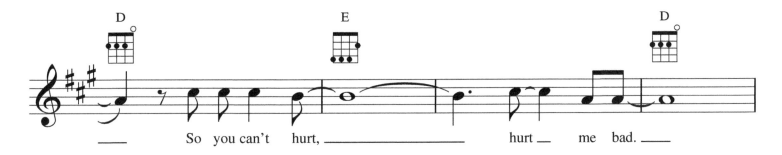

___ It is, it is, is a wa-ter-fall. ___ Oh. ___

___ So you can't hurt, ___ hurt ___ me bad. ___

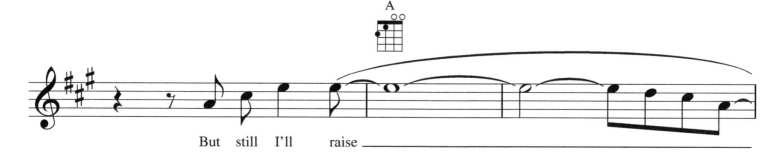

But still I'll raise

the flag. ___ Ooh.

Outro-Chorus

Ev - 'ry tear, ___ ev - 'ry tear, ___

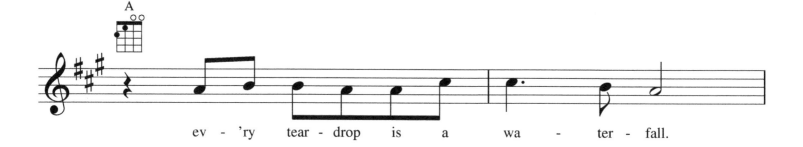

ev - 'ry tear-drop is a wa - ter - fall.

Ev - 'ry tear, __ ev - 'ry tear, __ ev - 'ry tear-drop is a

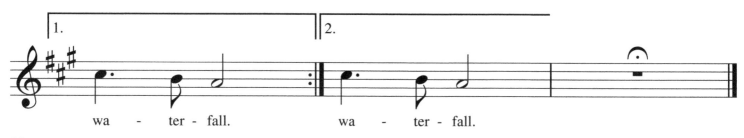

1. wa - ter - fall. 2. wa - ter - fall.

Don't Panic

Words and Music by Guy Berryman, Jon Buckland, Will Champion and Chris Martin

We live in a beau-ti-ful world, _____

yeah, we do, __ yeah, we do. We live in a beau-ti-ful world. _____

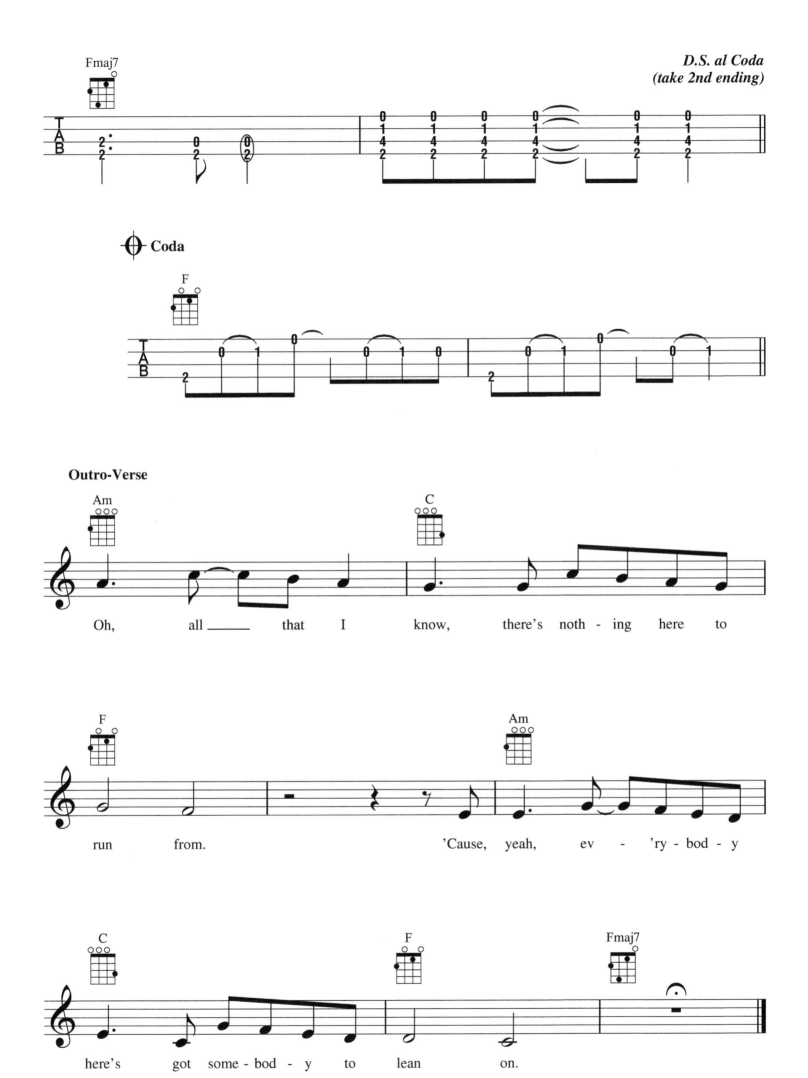

Fix You

Words and Music by Guy Berryman, Jon Buckland, Will Champion and Chris Martin

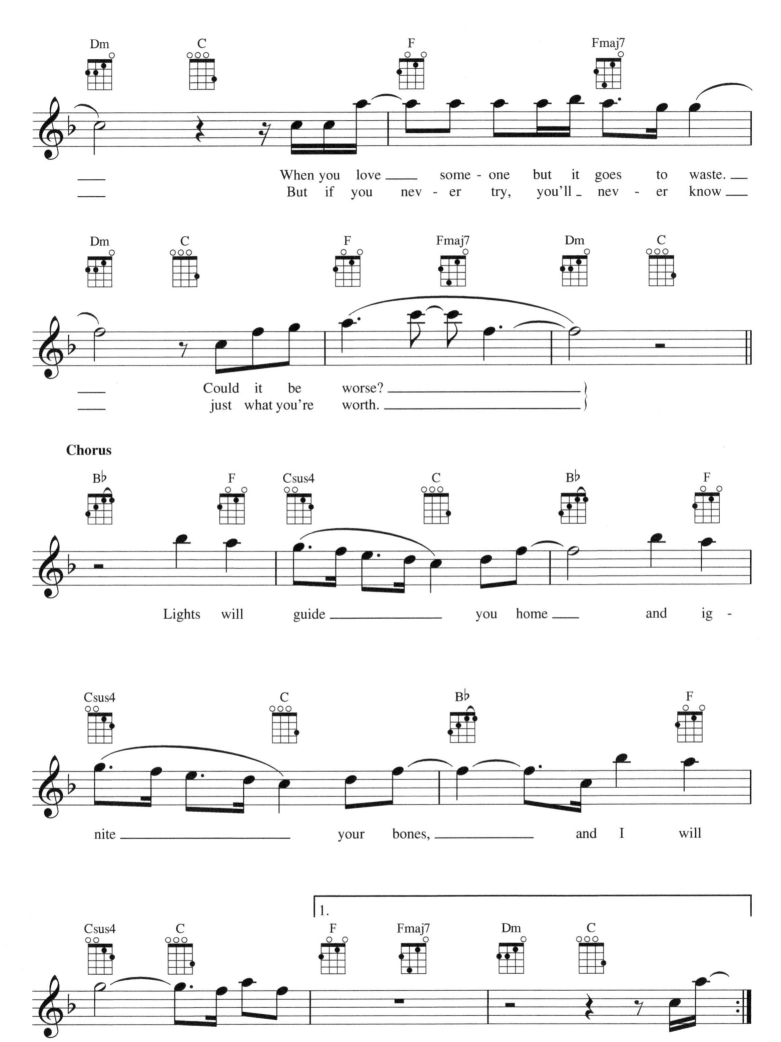

When you love ____ some - one but it goes to waste. ____
But if you nev - er try, you'll ____ nev - er know ____

____ Could it be worse? _____
____ just what you're worth. _____

Chorus

Lights will guide _____ you home ____ and ig -

nite _____ your bones, _____ and I will

1.

try _____ to fix you.   3. And high ____

2.

Interlude

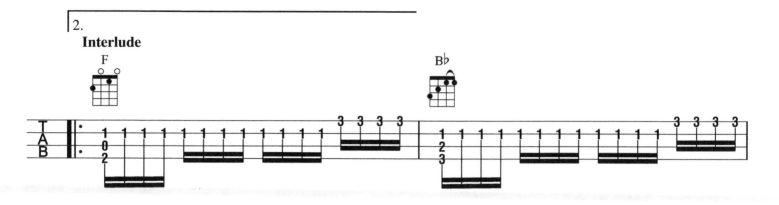

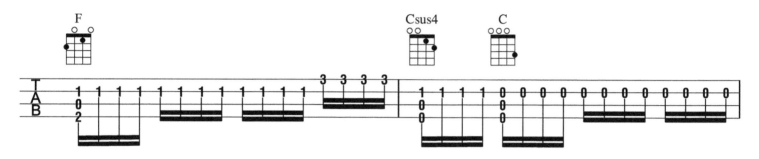

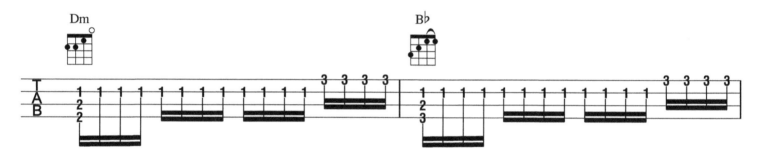

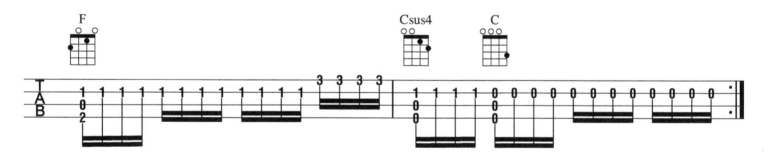

Bridge

Tears stream _ down your face _ when you lose some - thing

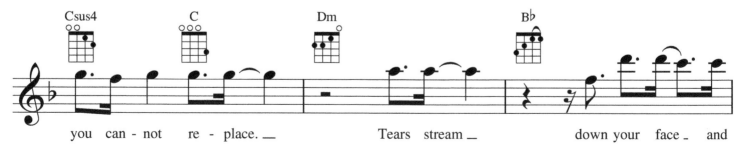

you can - not re - place. _ Tears stream _ down your face _ and

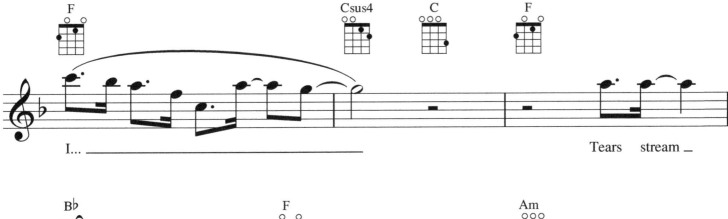

I... _____ Tears stream _

down your face. _ I prom - ise you I ___ will learn from my mis - takes. _

Tears stream _ down your face _ and I... _____

Outro-Chorus

___ Lights will guide _____ you home _

___ and ig - nite _____ your bones, ___ and I will

try _____ to fix you. ___

The Hardest Part

Words and Music by Guy Berryman, Jon Buckland, Will Champion and Chris Martin

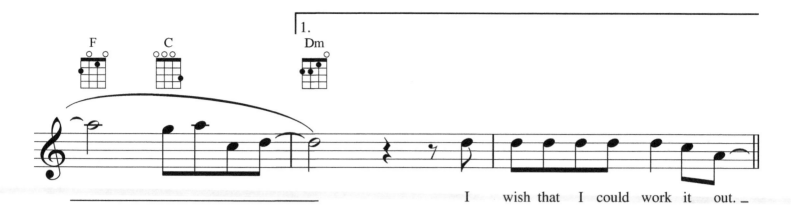

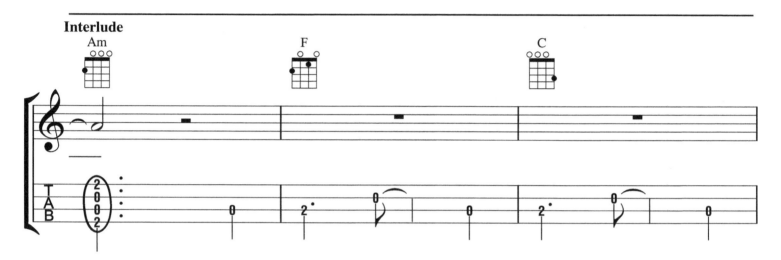

I wish that I could work it out.

Interlude

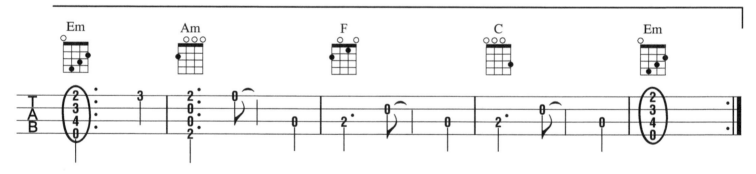

oh, and I,

D.C. al Coda

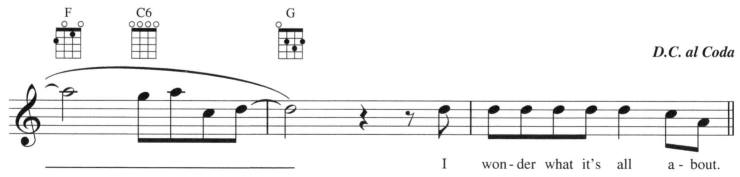

I won-der what it's all a-bout.

In My Place

Words and Music by Guy Berryman, Jon Buckland, Will Champion and Chris Martin

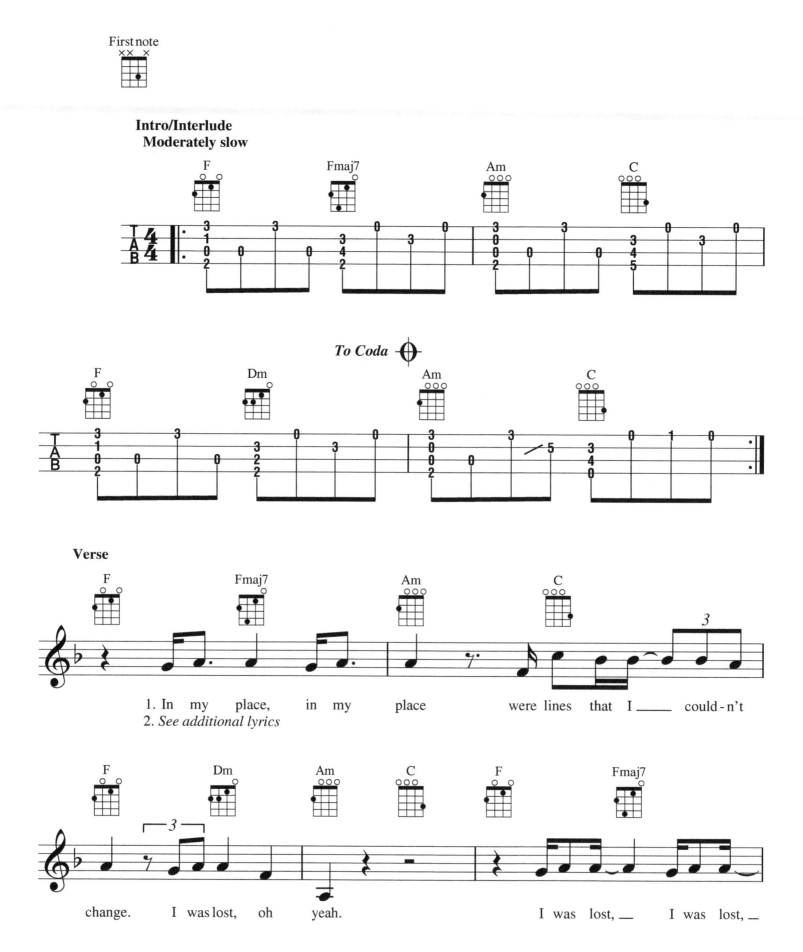

me,   to me, ___   to me. ___   Come on and sing it

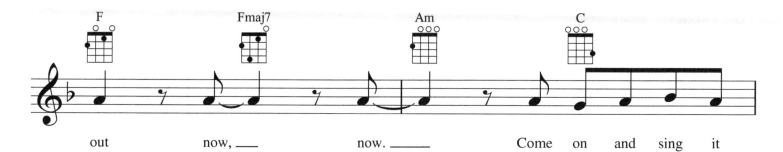

out   now, ___   now. ___   Come on and sing it

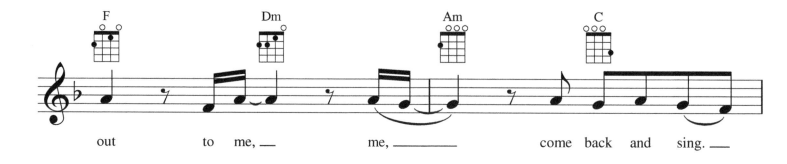

out   to me, ___   me, ___   come back and sing. ___

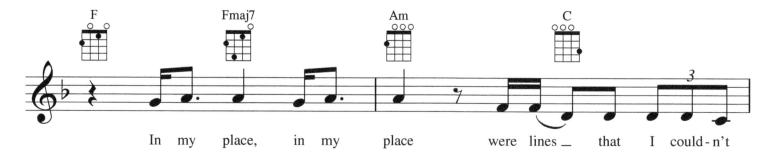

In my place,   in my   place   were lines _ that I could-n't

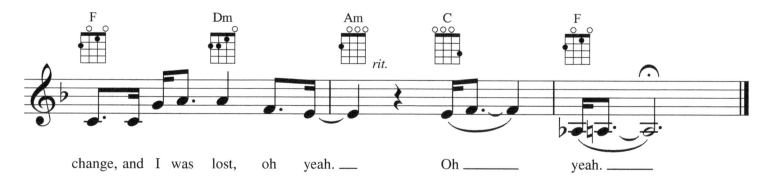

change, and I was lost,   oh   yeah. ___   Oh ___   yeah. ___

Additional Lyrics

2. I was scared, I was scared,
    Tired and under-prepared,
    But I'll wait for it.
    If you go, if you go
    And leave me down here on my own,
    Then I'll wait for you, yeah.

God Put a Smile Upon Your Face

Words and Music by Guy Berryman, Jon Buckland, Will Champion and Chris Martin

First note

Intro
Moderately

1. Where do we go?   No-bod-y knows. _____
2., 3. *See additional lyrics*

I've got to say   I'm on my way _____

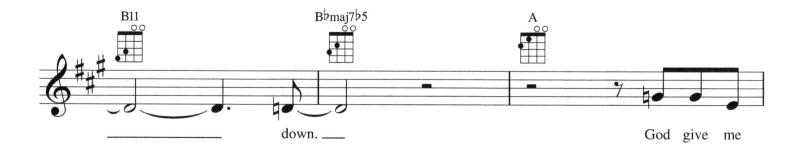

down. ___   God give me

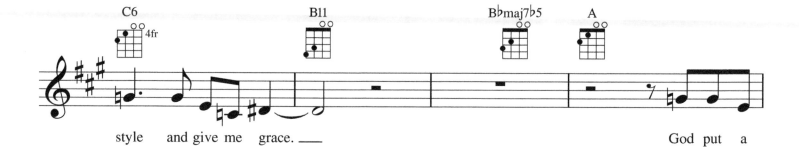

style   and give me   grace. ___   God put a

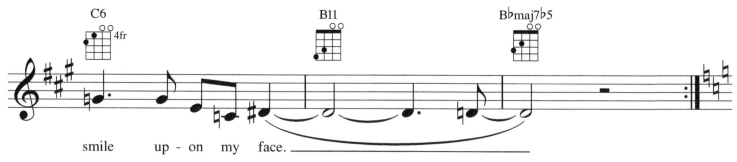

smile   up - on   my   face. ___

Chorus

Ah, _____ when you work ___ it out, ___ I'm worse ___

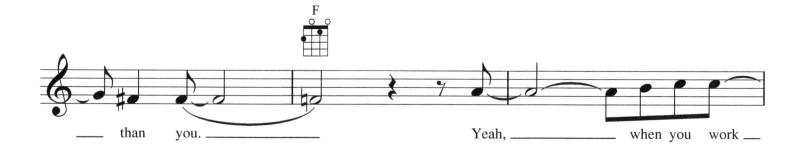

___ than   you. _____   Yeah, _____ when you work ___

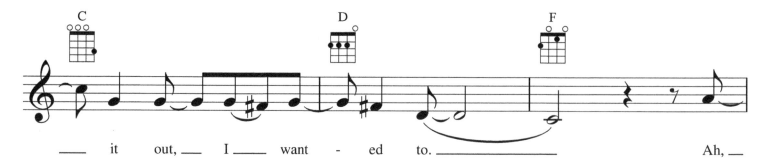

___ it out, ___ I ___ want - ed to. _____   Ah, ___

when you work out where to draw the line,

your guess is as good as mine.

Interlude

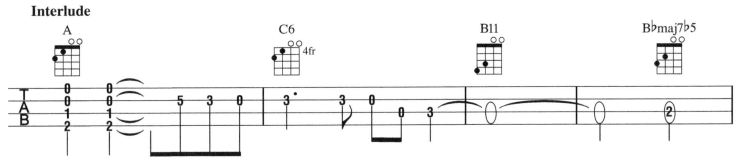

D.S. al Coda
(no repeat)

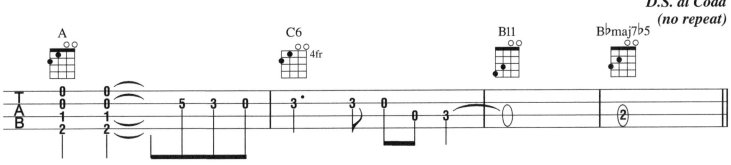

⊕ Coda

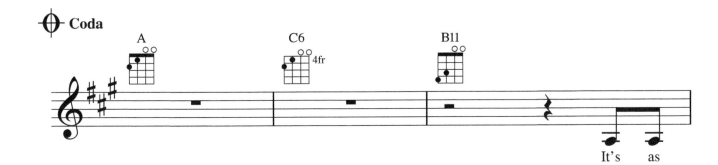

It's as

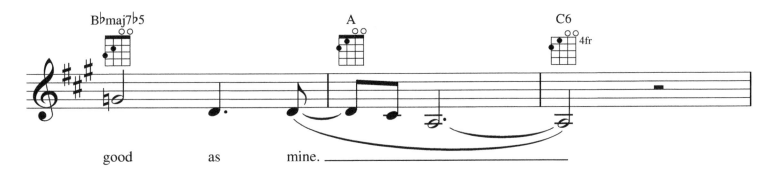

good as mine.

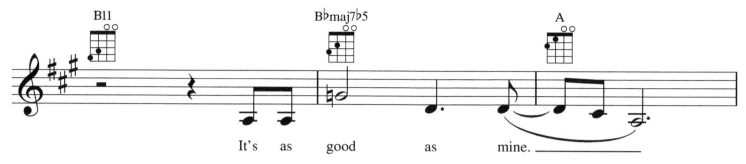

It's   as   good   as   mine. _____

It's   as   good   as   mine. __

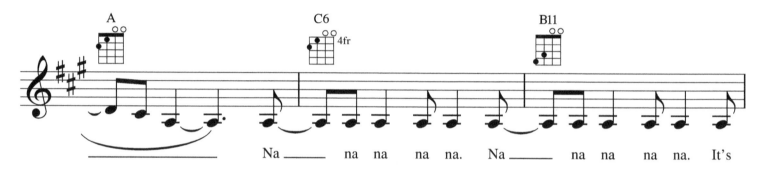

_____   Na ____ na na na na.   Na ____ na na na na.   It's

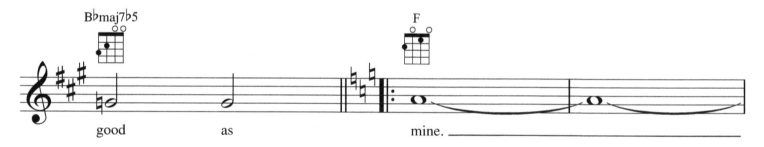

good   as   mine. _____

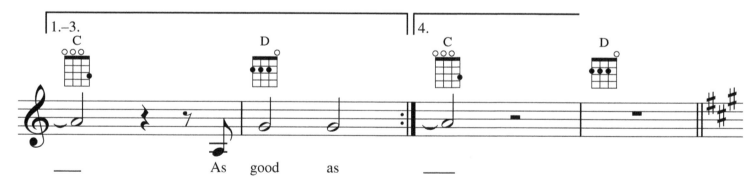

___   As good as   ___

Outro-Verse

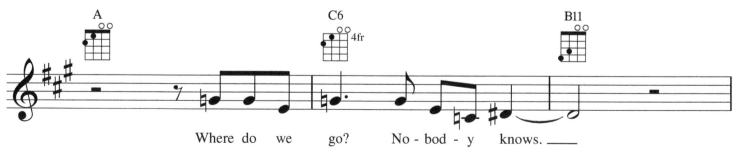

Where do we go?   No - bod - y   knows. ___

Don't ev - er say you're on your way ___

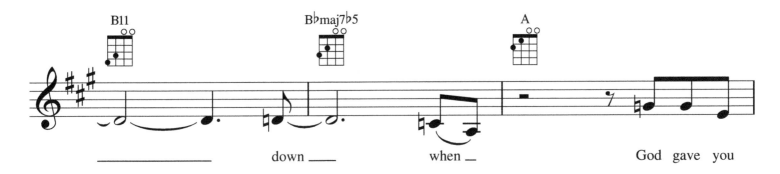

_____ down ___ when ___ God gave you

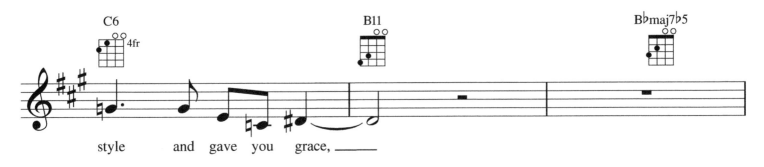

style and gave you grace, _____

and put a smile up - on your face. _____

Additional Lyrics

2. Where do we go to draw the line?
   I've got to say I wasted all your time, honey, honey.
   Where do I go to fall from grace?
   God put a smile upon your face, yeah.

3. Where do we go? Nobody knows.
   Don't ever say you're on your way down when
   God gave you style and gave you grace,
   And put a smile upon your face.

Chorus
Now, when you work it out...

Life in Technicolor II

Words and Music by Guy Berryman, Jon Buckland, Will Champion and Chris Martin

ing. _____ There's a cold ___ war ___ com - ing, on the ra -

- di - o ___ I heard. ___ Ba - by, it's a

vi - 'lent ___ world. ___ Oh, ___

𝄋 **Chorus**

love, ___ don't let _____ me go. ___ Won't you take _

_____ me where the street lights _ glow? _____ I can hear _

___ it ___ com - ing, { I can hear ___ the si - ren's sound; _
{ like a ser - e - nade _ of sound; _

now my   feet ___ won't touch ___   the ground. ___

Interlude

Verse

___   came ___ a-creep-ing,   oh, and time's ___   a load-ed   gun. ___

___   Ev-'ry   road _____   is   a   ray ___   of ___   light. ___

_____   It   goes   on, _____

time on-ly ___ can lead ___ you on. ___ Still it's _____ such a beau - ti - ful

D.S. al Coda   **Coda**

night.   Oh, ___   ___

Outro

Grav -

- i - ty, ___ re - lease ___ me, and don't ev - er hold ___ me down. ___

___ Now my feet ___ won't touch ___ the ground. ___

Lost!

Words and Music by Guy Berryman, Jon Buckland, Will Champion and Chris Martin

locked. Oh, _____ and I'm _____ just wait-ing till the shine wears off. _____

off. Oh, _____ and I'm _____ just wait-ing till the fir - ing's stopped. _

_____

_____

Oh, _____ and I'm _

_____ just wait-ing till the shine wears off. _____

D.S. al Coda

Coda

End instrumental Oh, _____ and I'm _____ just

(Vocal 1st time only)

Outro

wait-ing till the shine wears off. _____

Oh, _____ and I'm _

Repeat and fade

_____ just wait-ing till the shine wears off. _____

Speed of Sound

Words and Music by Guy Berryman, Jon Buckland, Will Champion and Chris Martin

_____ what it feels _____ like? _____ Where to, where do I go? _____ If you nev-er try, _

_____ then you'll nev-er know. _____ How long do I have to climb _

_____ up on the side _____ of this moun-tain of mine? _____

Interlude

2. Look
3. I -

but be - fore I see ____ things the right way up. ____
but oth - ers are puz - zles, __ puz - zl - in' me.

Pre-Chorus

All that noise ___ and all that sound. __

All those plac - es I ___ got found. __ And

𝄋 Chorus

birds go fly - in' at the speed of sound __ to show ya how it all be - gan. __

___ Birds ___ came fly - in' from the un - der - ground. _ If you could

To Coda ⊕ 1.

see it, then you'd un - der - stand. _____

44

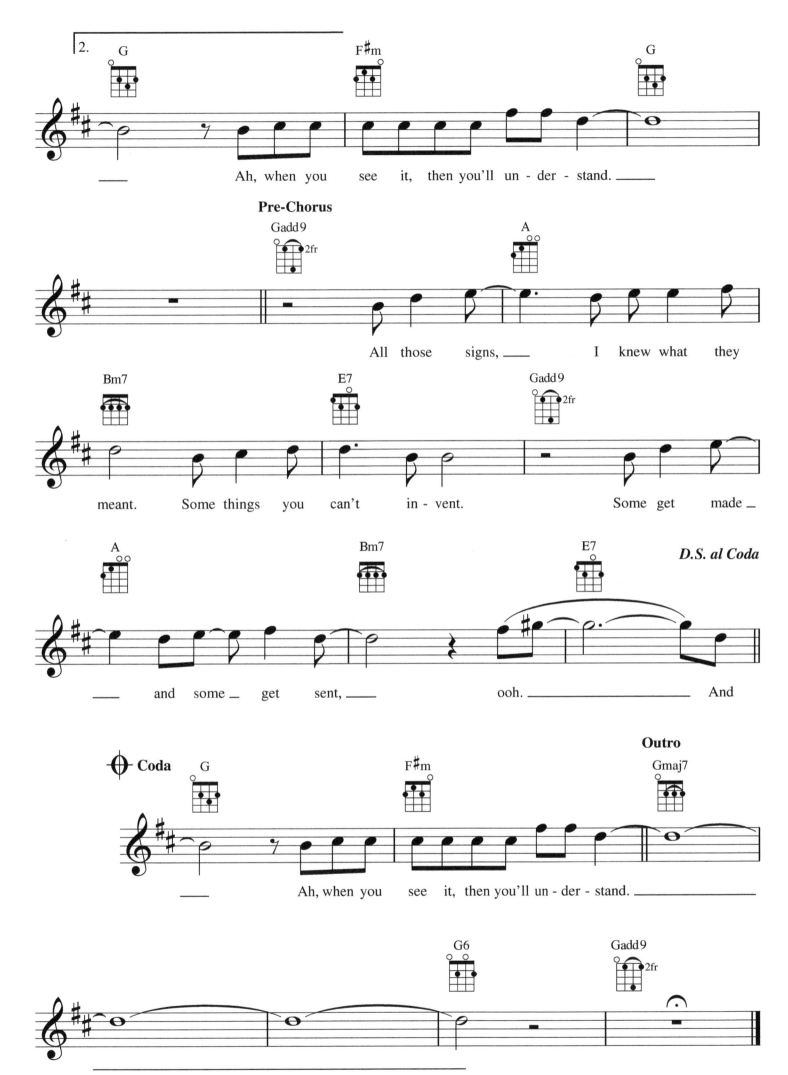

The Scientist

Words and Music by Guy Berryman, Jon Buckland, Will Champion and Chris Martin

-crets and ask me your ques - tions, oh, let's go back to the start. _____

_____ Run - ning in cir - cles, com-ing up tails, _____ heads on a si-

Chorus

- lence a - part. _____ No - bod - y said _____ it was eas - y. _____

Oh, it's _____ such a shame _____ for us to part. _____ No - bod - y said _____

_____ it was eas - y. _____ No _____ one ev - er said _____ it would be {this _ hard. _ / so _ hard. _

Oh, take me } back to the start. _____
I'm go - ing }

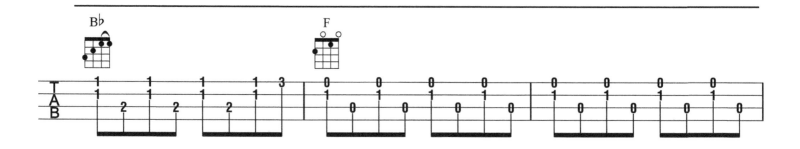

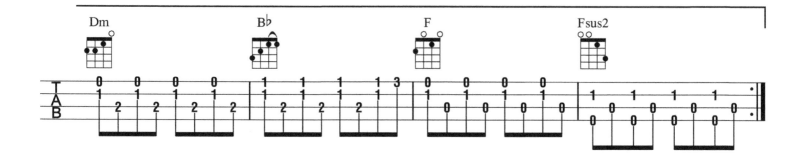

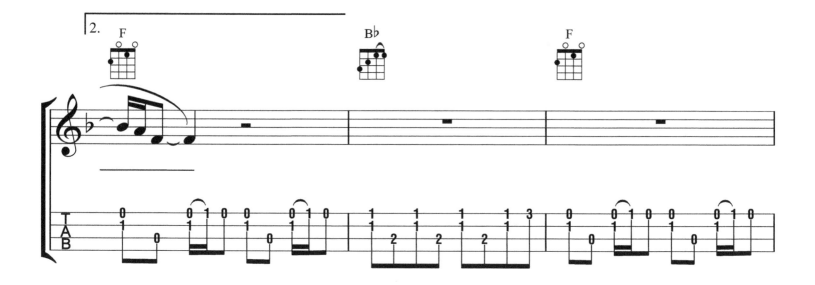

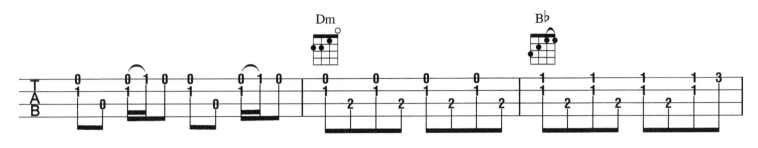

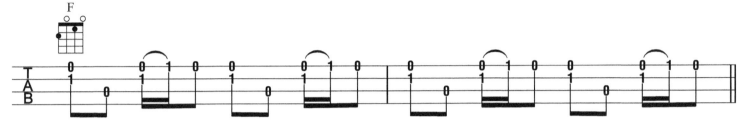

Outro

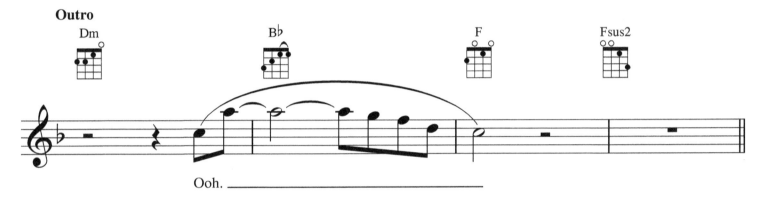

Ooh.

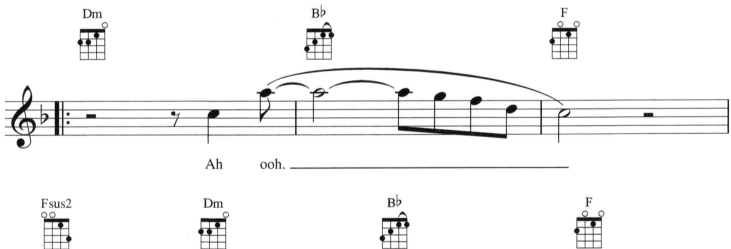

Ah   ooh.

Ah   ooh.

Additional Lyrics

2. I was just guessing at numbers and figures,
Pulling the puzzles apart.
Questions of science, science and progress
Do not speak as loud as my heart.
And tell me you love me, come back and haunt me.
Oh, and I rush to the start.
Running in circles, chasing our tails,
Coming back as we are.

Shiver

Words and Music by Guy Berryman, Jon Buckland, Will Champion and Chris Martin

First note

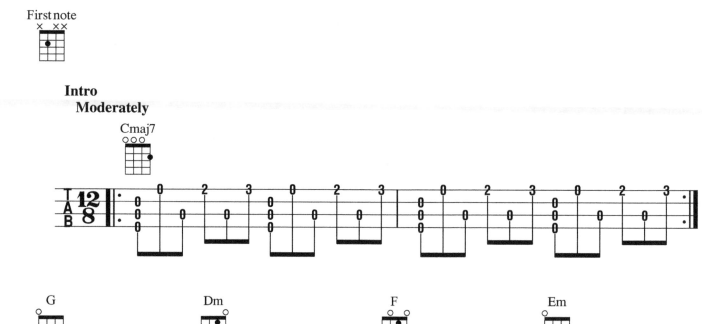

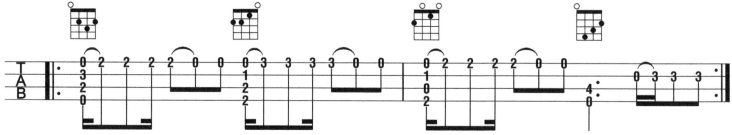

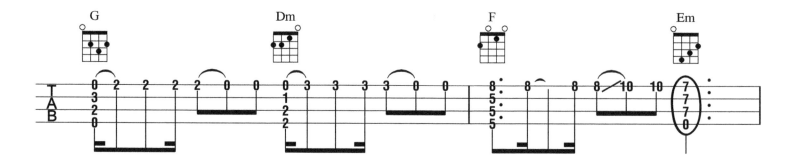

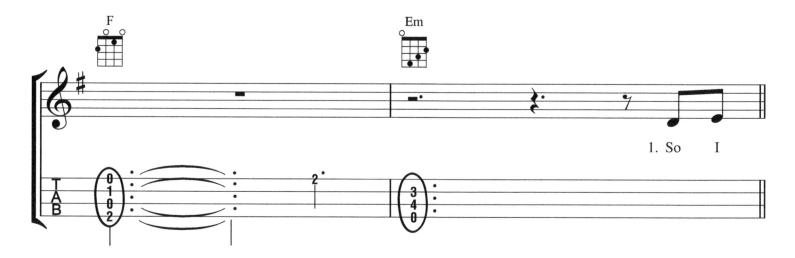

Verse

look in your di - rec - tion, but you pay me no at - ten - tion, ___ do you? ___
(2.) *See additional lyrics*

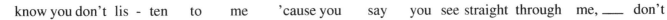

And I

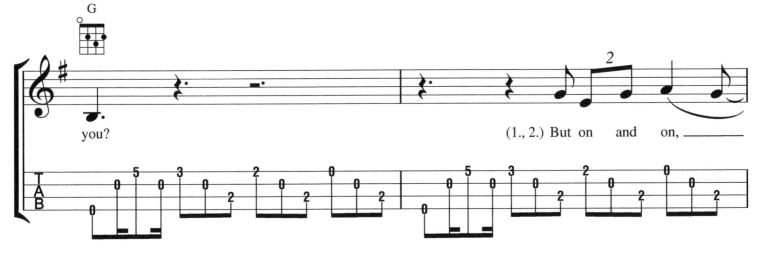

know you don't lis - ten to me 'cause you say you see straight through me, ___ don't

you? ___ (1., 2.) But on and on, ___

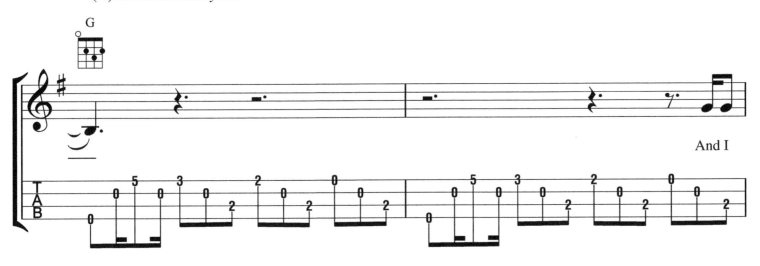

___ from the mo - ment I wake ___ to the mo - ment I sleep, _

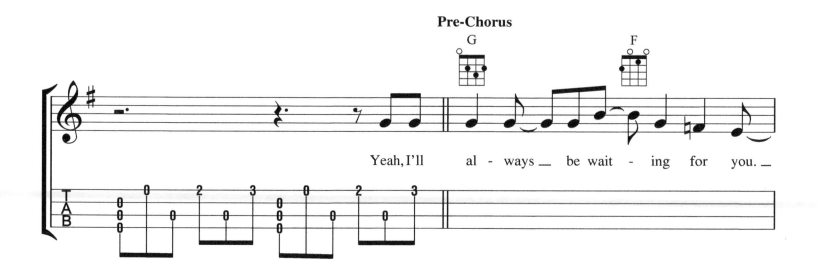

Pre-Chorus

Yeah, I'll al - ways __ be wait - ing for you. __

__ Yeah, I'll al - ways __ be wait - ing for you. __

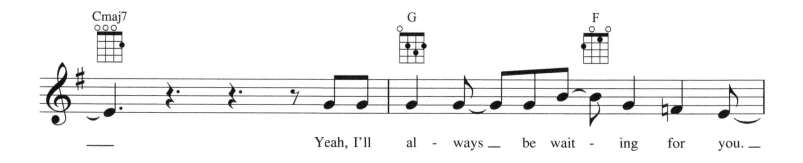

__ Yeah, I'll al - ways __ be wait - ing for you. __

__ For __ you I will al - ways __ be wait - ing. And it's

Chorus

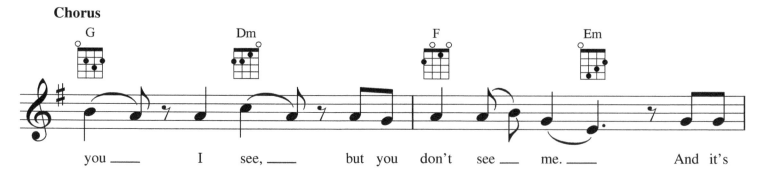

you __ I see, __ but you don't see __ me. __ And it's

54

you ___ I hear, ___ oh, so loud and so clear. ___ I'll sing it

loud _____ and clear. _____ And I'll

al - ways ___ be wait - ing ___ for you. So I

Outro-Verse

look in your di - rec - tion, but you pay me no at - ten - tion. And you

know how much I need you, but you nev - er e - ven see me. ___

Additional Lyrics

2. So you know how much I need you.
But you never even see me, do you?
And is this my final chance of getting you?

Paradise

Words and Music by Guy Berryman, Jon Buckland, Will Champion, Chris Martin and Brian Eno

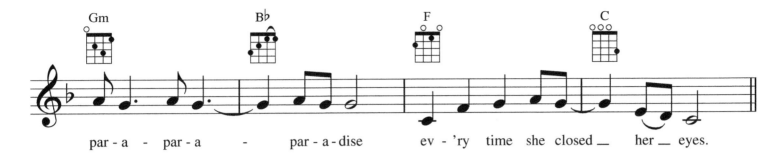

par - a - par - a - par - a - dise   ev - 'ry time she closed __ her __ eyes.

Interlude

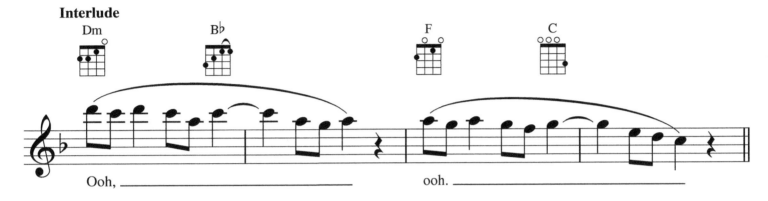

Ooh, _____   ooh. _____

Verse

2. When she was just a girl, _____   she ex - pect - ed the world. __

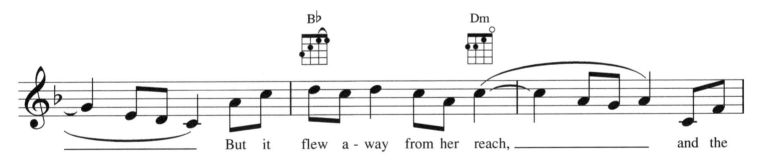

_____   But it flew a - way from her reach, _____   and the

bul - lets catch in her teeth. _____   Life goes on, it gets __

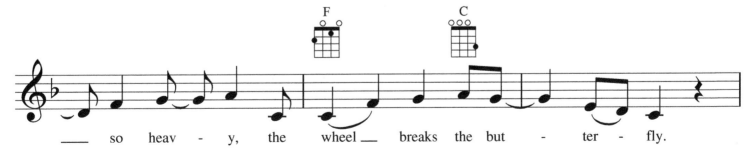

__ so heav - y, the wheel __ breaks the but - ter - fly.

par - a - par - a - par - a - dise, par - a - par - a -

- par - a - dise, par - a - par - a - par - a - dise.

Bridge

Oh, _____ oh. _____ La, la, _____ la, la, la,

la, la, _____ la, la, la, la, la, _____ la, la, la, _____ la, la. _____ And so ly -

- ing un - der - neath _____ those storm - y skies, _____

she said, "Oh, _____ I know the

sun   must   set   to   rise. _____   This could be   par - a - par - a -

- par - a - dise,   par - a - par - a - par - a - dise,   could be

par - a - par - a - par - a - dise.   Oh, _____ oh. _

Outro

_____ Ooh, _____

ooh. _____   Ooh, _____

_____   ooh. _____

Talk

Words and Music by Guy Berryman, Jon Buckland, Will Champion, Chris Martin, Ralf Huetter, Emil Schult and Karl Bartos

First note

Intro
Moderately fast

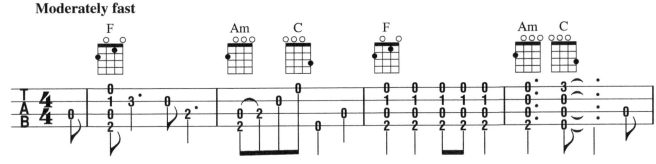

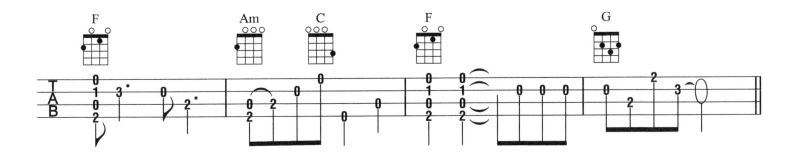

Verse

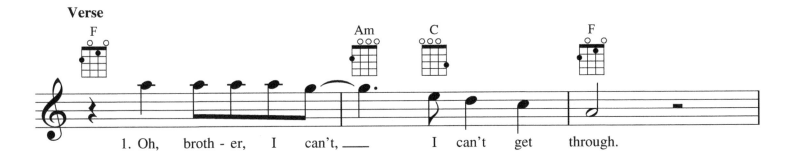

1. Oh, broth-er, I can't, ___ I can't get through.

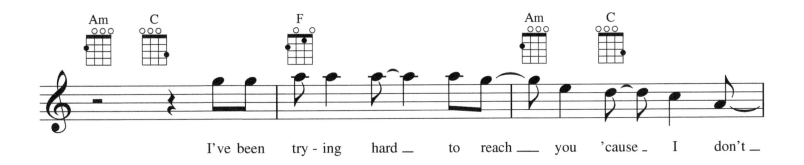

I've been try-ing hard ___ to reach ___ you 'cause ___ I don't ___

know what to do. ___ Oh, broth- er, I can't ___

be - lieve it's true. I'm so

scared a - bout the fu - ture and ___ I want ___

___ to talk to you. ___ Oh, I want ___ to talk to you. ___

You could

𝄋 **Chorus**

(1., D.S.) take a pic - ture of some-thing you see. ___
(D.S.S.) don't know where you're go - ing and you want to talk. ___

In the fu-ture, where will I be? __
You feel like you're go-ing where you've been be-fore. __

You could climb a lad-der
You'll tell an-y-one who'll lis-ten, but you

To Coda 2 ⊕

up to the sun, __ or
feel ig-nored. __ And

To Coda 1 ⊕

write a song no-bod-y had sung __ or do __ some-thing that's

nev-er been done. __

Verse

2. Are you lost __ or in-com-plete?

Do you feel like ___ a puz - zle, you ___ can't find ___

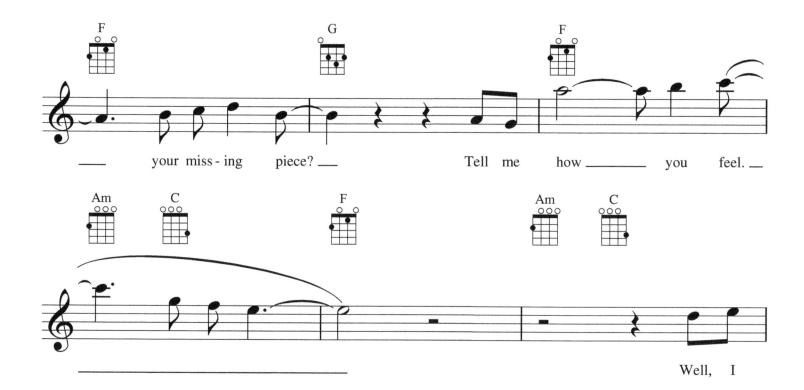

___ your miss - ing piece? ___ Tell me how _____ you feel.

_____

Well, I

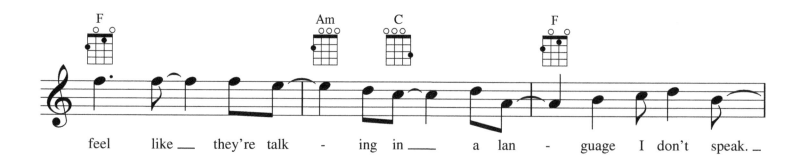

feel like ___ they're talk - ing in ___ a lan - guage I don't speak. ___

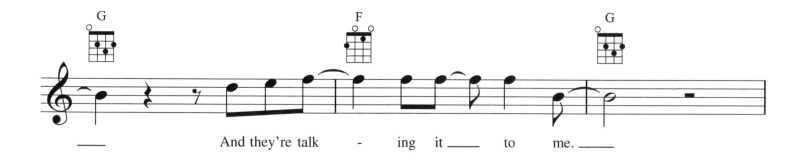

___ And they're talk - ing it ___ to me. ___

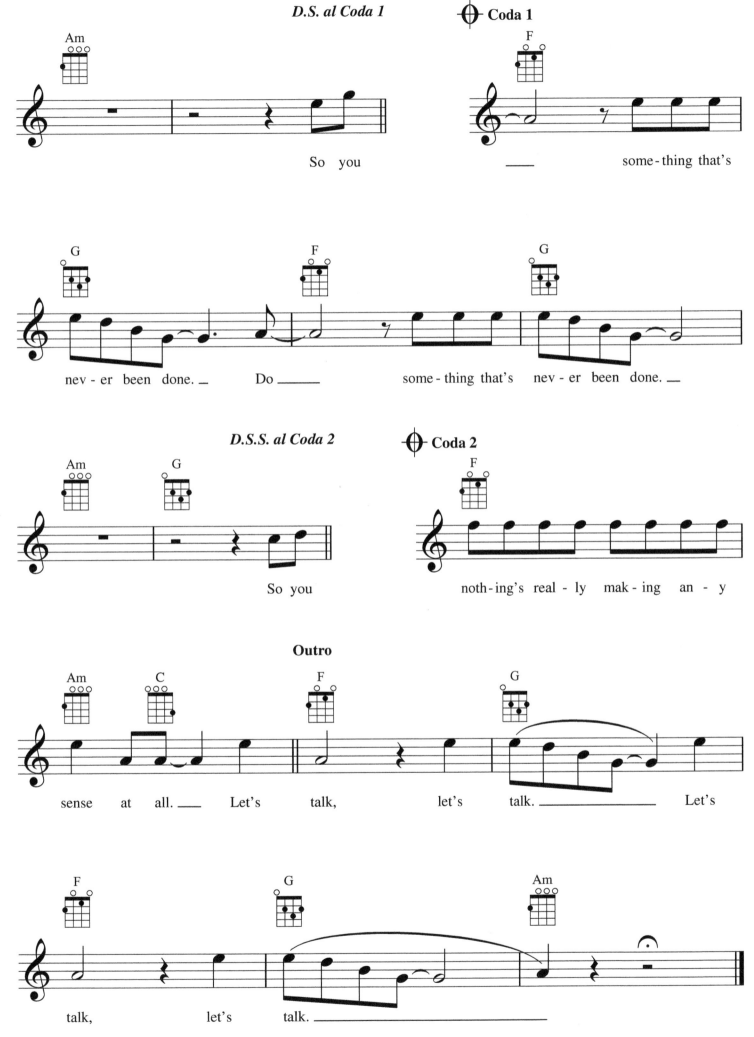

Trouble

Words and Music by Guy Berryman, Jon Buckland, Will Champion and Chris Martin

First note

Intro
Moderately slow

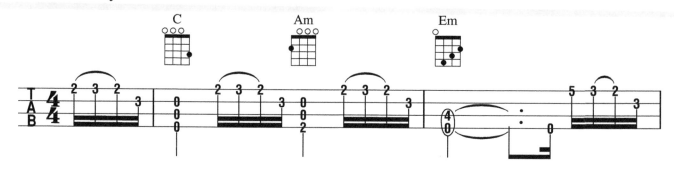

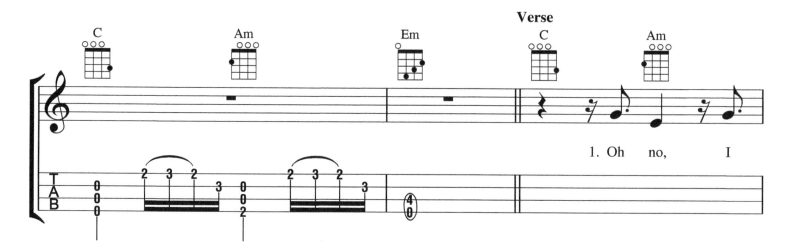

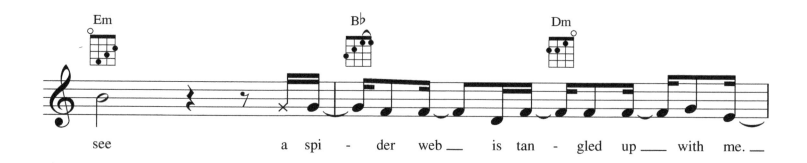

see   a spi - der web   is tan - gled up   with me.

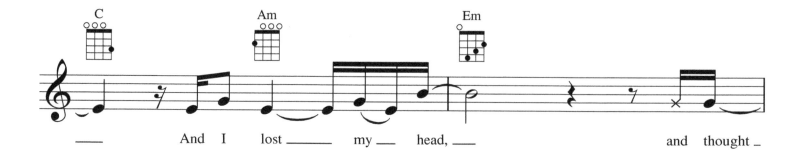

     And I lost   my   head,   and thought

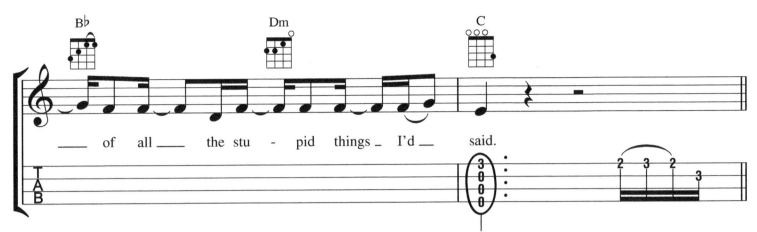

_____ of all _____ the stu - pid things _ I'd _____ said.

Interlude

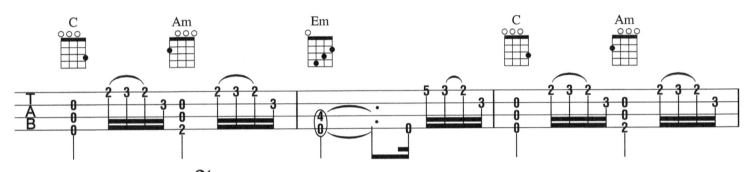

Verse

2. Oh no, what's this? A spi -
3. *See additional lyrics*

- der web _ and I'm caught in the mid - dle. So I turned to _ run, _

_____ and thought _ of all _____ the stu - pid things _ I'd _____

Additional Lyrics

3. Oh no, I see a spider web and it's me in the middle.
So I twist and turn, but here am I in my little bubble.

Viva la Vida

Words and Music by Guy Berryman, Jon Buckland, Will Champion and Chris Martin

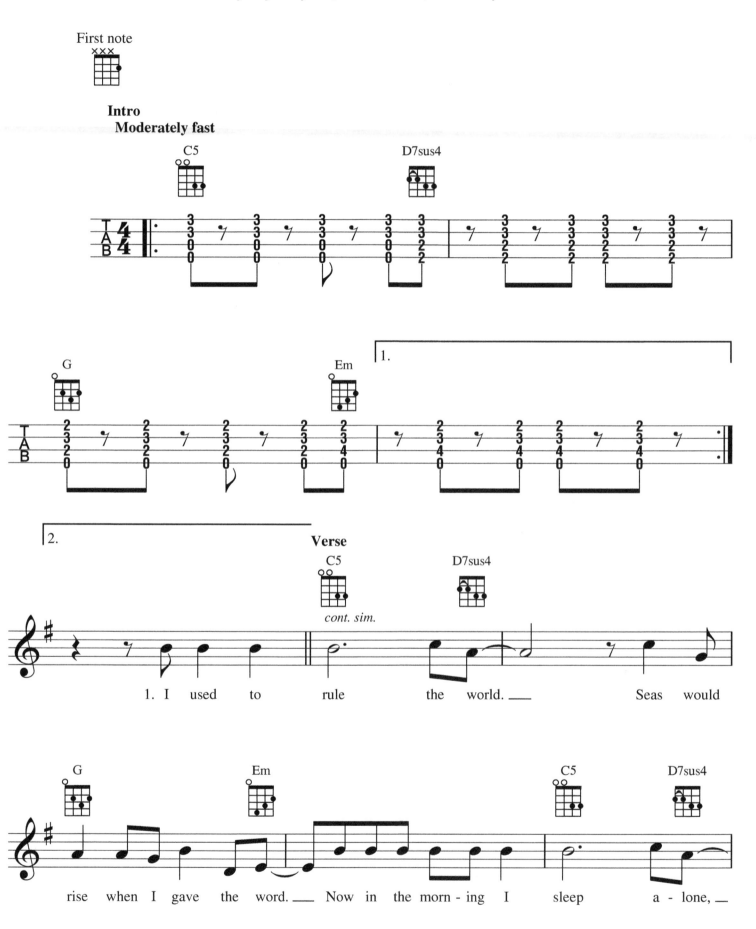

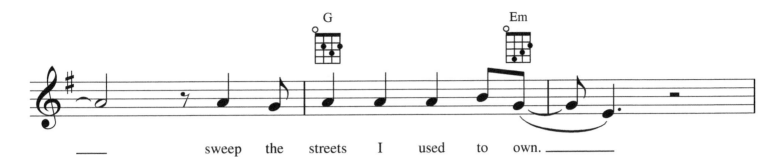

sweep the streets I used to own. _____

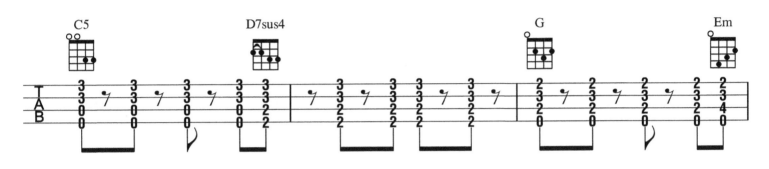

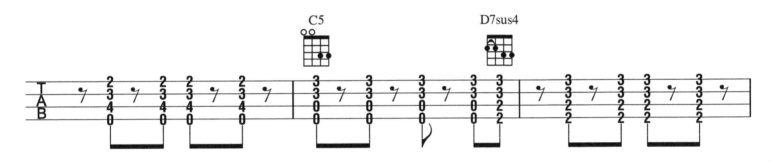

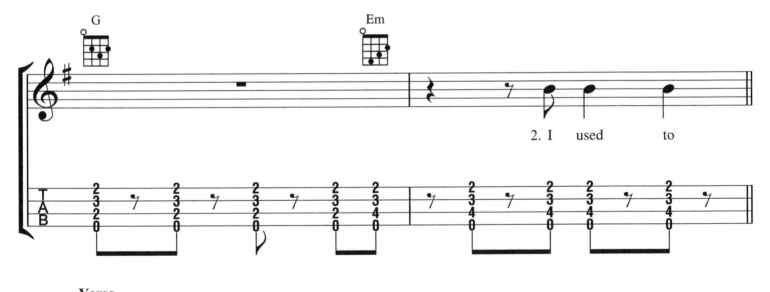

2. I used to

Verse

roll the dice, ____ feel the fear in my en - e - mies' eyes. __
____ wind blew down the doors to let me in. __

Lis - ten as the crowd _____ would sing, _____
Shat - tered win - dows and the sound _____ of drums. _

_____
_____

"Now the old king is dead, _____ long live
Peo - ple could - n't be - lieve _____ what I'd _____

the king." One min - ute I held the key, _____ next the
_____ be - come. Rev - o - lu - tion - ar - ies wait _____ for my

walls were closed on me. And I dis - cov - ered that my cas - tles stand _
head on a sil - ver plate. _____ Just a pup - pet on a lone - ly string. _

_____ up - on pil - lars of salt _ and pil - lars of sand. _____ I
_____ Oh, _ who would ev - er wan - na be king? _____ I

72

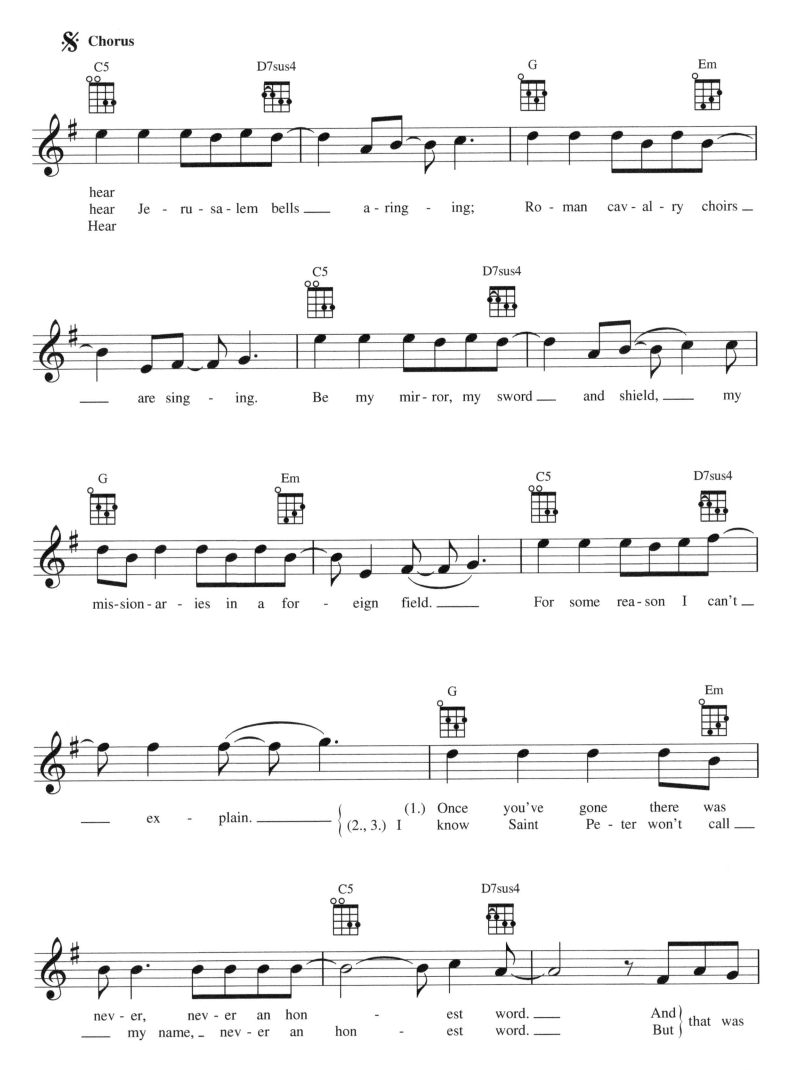

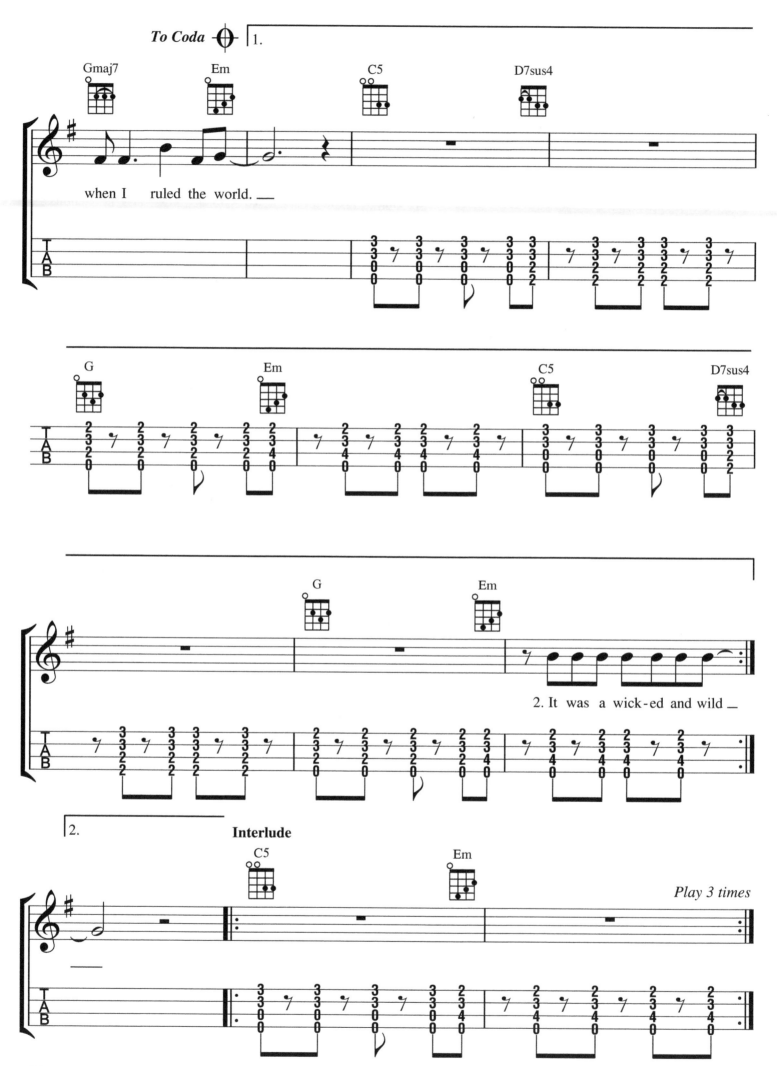

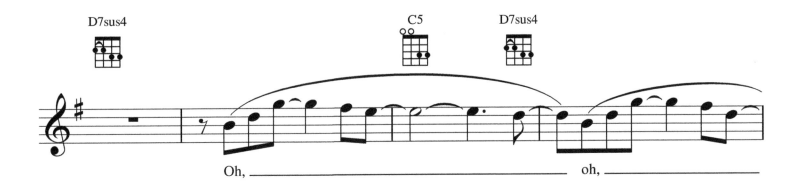

Oh, _____ oh, _____

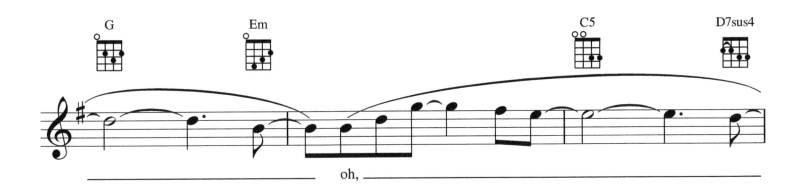

_____ oh, _____

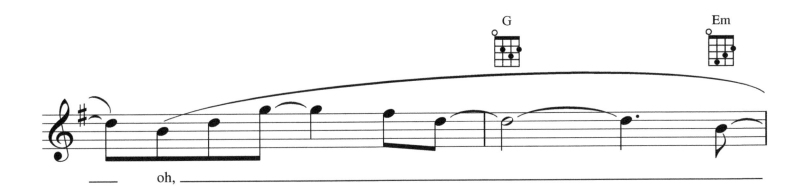

___ oh, _____

D.S. al Coda   ⊕ **Coda**

___ oh. _____

Outro   *Repeat and fade*

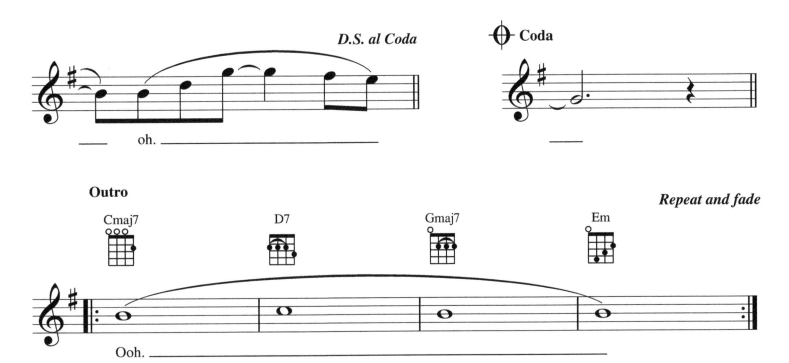

Ooh. _____

A Warning Sign

Words and Music by Guy Berryman, Jon Buckland, Will Champion and Chris Martin

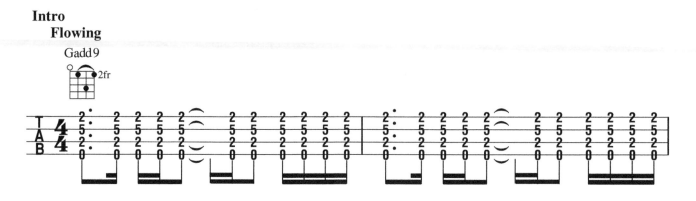

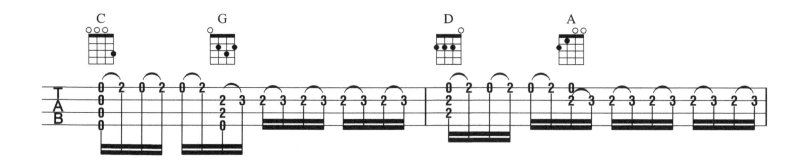

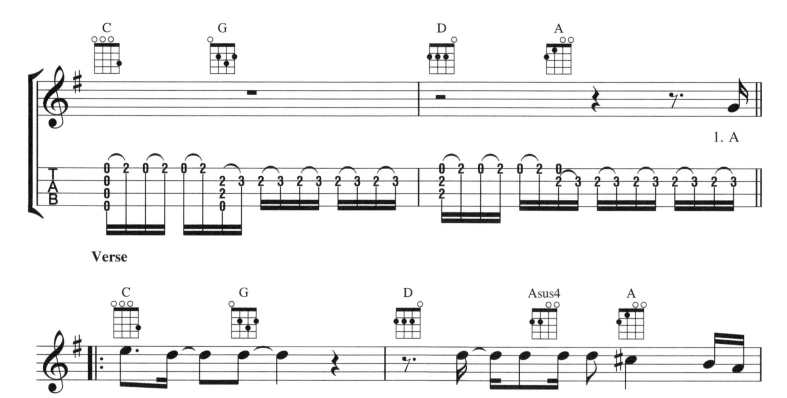

warn - ing ___ sign, ___   I ___ missed the good part,   then I

2. *See additional lyrics*

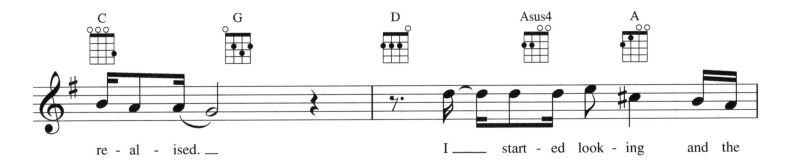

re - al - ised. ___   I ___ start - ed look - ing   and the

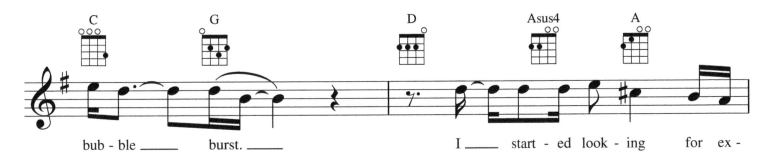

bub - ble ___ burst. ___   I ___ start - ed look - ing   for ex -

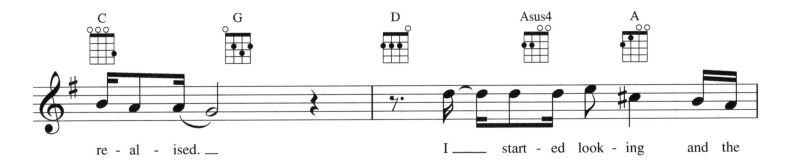

cus - es. ___

Pre-Chorus

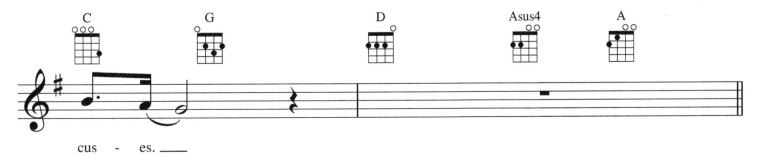

Come on ___ in, ___   I've ___ got to tell you   what a

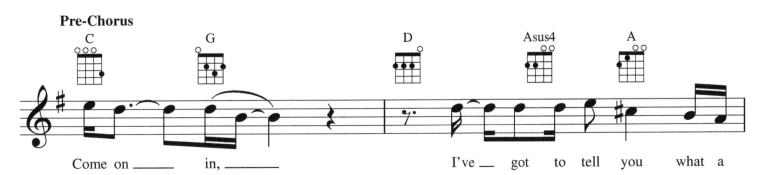

state I'm ___ in. ___   I've ___ got to tell you   in my

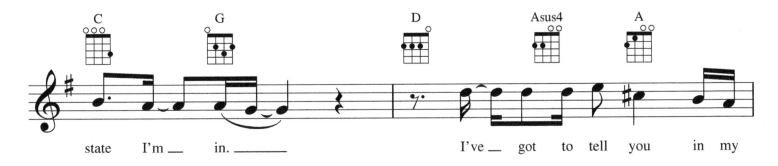

loud - est ___ tones ___   that I ___ start - ed look - ing   for a

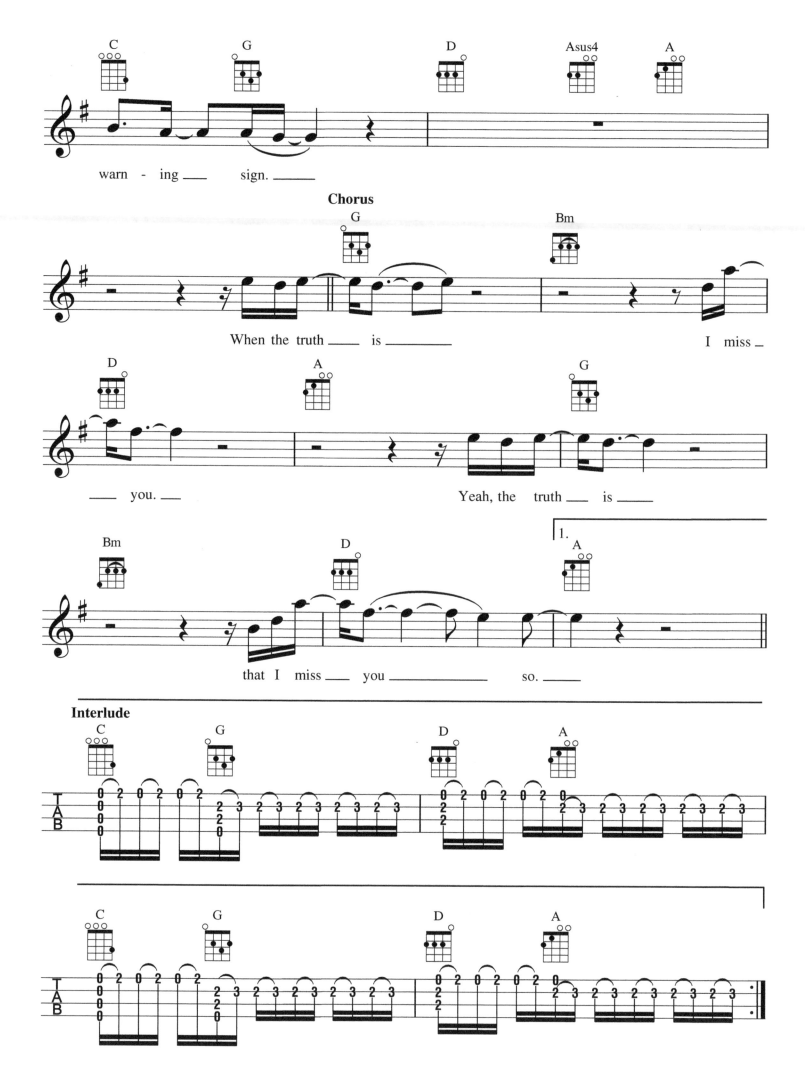

warn - ing ____ sign. ____

Chorus

When the truth ____ is _____ I miss ____

____ you. ____ Yeah, the truth ____ is ____

that I miss ____ you _____ so. ____

Interlude

Additional Lyrics

2. A warning sign,
   You came back to haunt me,
   And I realised that you were an island,
   And I passed you by
   When you were an island to discover.

Yellow

Words and Music by Guy Berryman, Jon Buckland, Will Champion and Chris Martin

First note

Intro
Moderate Rock

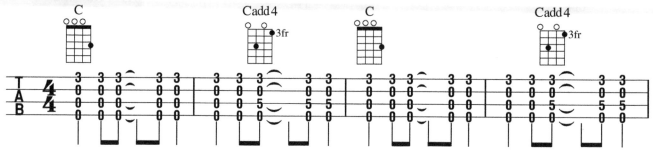

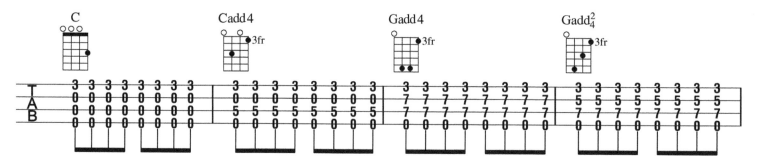

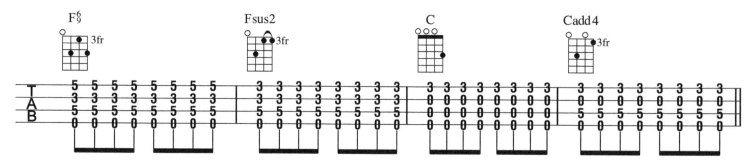

Verse

1. Look at the stars; look how they shine for _____ you

and ev-'ry-thing you __ do. ___ Yeah, they were all __ yel-low. _

Verse

2. I came a-long;   I wrote a song for _____ you
3. I swam a-cross;   I jumped a-cross for _____ you.

and all the things you __ do, ____   and it was called _ "Yel-low." _
Oh, what a thing to __ do, ____   'cause you were all ____ yel-low. _

I drew a line, ____   So then I took my _____ turn.
        I drew a line for _____ you.

Oh, what a thing to have done; __   and it was all ____ yel-low. _
Oh, what a thing to __ do; __   and they was all ____ yel-low. _

Bridge

Your skin, _____

____ oh yeah, your skin and bones   turn - ing _____ to some-thing beau - ti - ful

And you ___ know _____ { you know I love you so, ___
                                   { for you I bleed my - self

___ dry,   you know I love you so.
                for you I bleed my - self

Interlude

dry.

It's

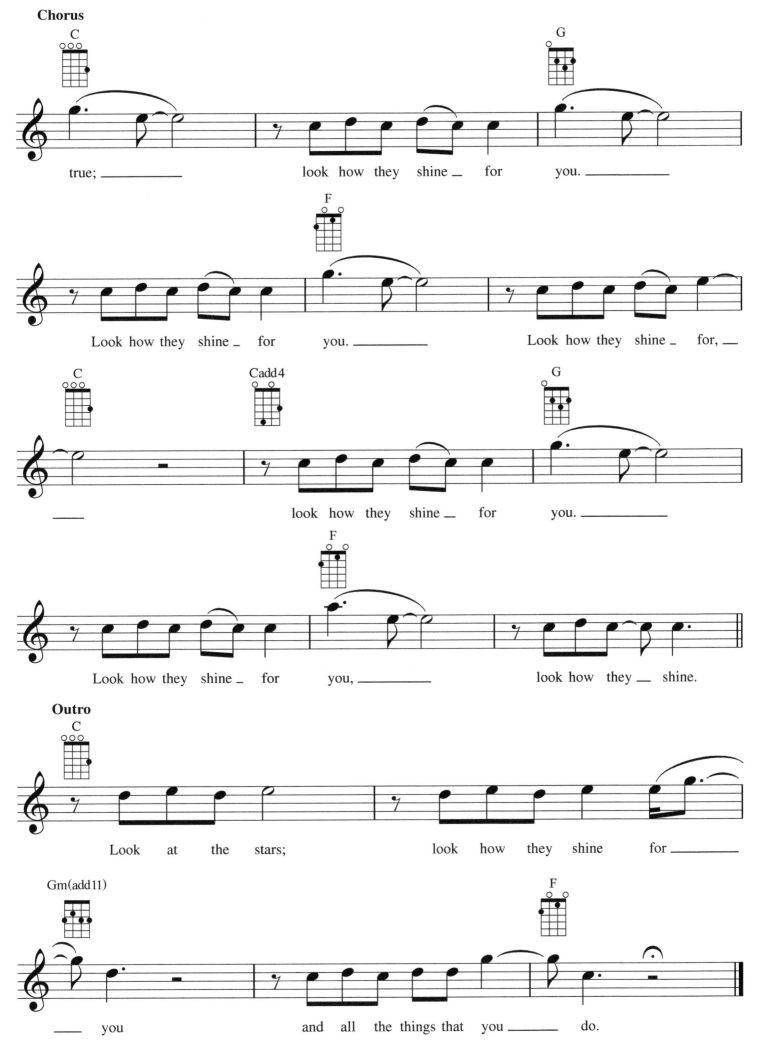

Chorus

true; _____ look how they shine _ for you. _____

Look how they shine _ for you. _____ Look how they shine _ for, __

__ look how they shine _ for you. _____

Look how they shine _ for you, _____ look how they _ shine.

Outro

Look at the stars; look how they shine for _____

__ you and all the things that you _____ do.

Violet Hill

Words and Music by Guy Berryman, Jon Buckland, Will Champion and Chris Martin

low. _____
loft. _____

When the fu - ture's ar - chi - tec - tured by a car -
Bur - y me ___ in hon - or when I'm dead ___
___ to be ___ a sol - dier with the cap -

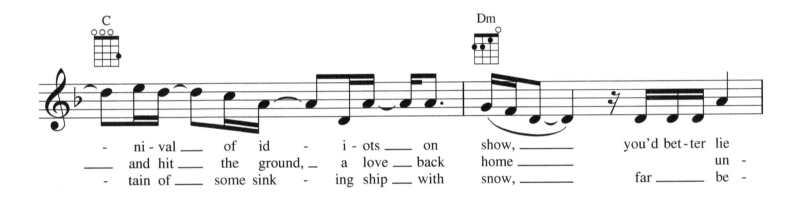

- ni - val ___ of id - i - ots ___ on show, _____ you'd bet-ter lie
___ and hit ___ the ground, a love ___ back home _____ un -
- tain of ___ some sink - ing ship ___ with snow, _____ far _____ be -

Chorus

low. _____
folds. _____
low. _____

If you love me, ___ won't you let ___ me ___ know? ___

|1. |2.   *D.S. al Coda*|

To Coda ⊕

_____   2. Was a long ___   3. I don't want ___

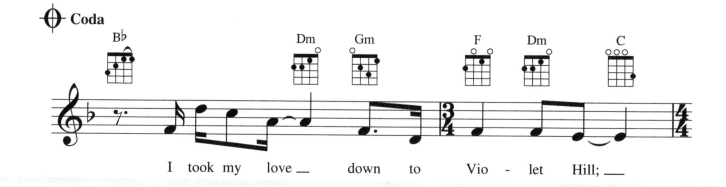

I took my love __ down to Vio - let Hill; __

there we sat __ in snow. All that time, __ she was

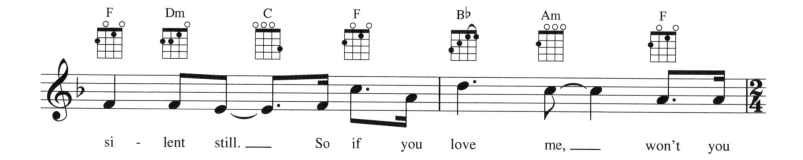

si - lent still. __ So if you love me, __ won't you

let __ me know? __ If you

love me, __ won't you let __ me know? __

HAL•LEONARD® UKULELE PLAY-ALONG

1. POP HITS
00701451 Book/CD Pack $15.99

3. HAWAIIAN FAVORITES
00701453 Book/Online Audio $14.99

4. CHILDREN'S SONGS
00701454 Book/Online Audio $14.99

5. CHRISTMAS SONGS
00701696 Book/CD Pack $12.99

6. LENNON & MCCARTNEY
00701723 Book/Online Audio $12.99

7. DISNEY FAVORITES
00701724 Book/Online Audio $14.99

8. CHART HITS
00701745 Book/CD Pack $15.99

9. THE SOUND OF MUSIC
00701784 Book/CD Pack $14.99

10. MOTOWN
00701964 Book/CD Pack $12.99

11. CHRISTMAS STRUMMING
00702458 Book/Online Audio $12.99

12. BLUEGRASS FAVORITES
00702584 Book/CD Pack $12.99

13. UKULELE SONGS
00702599 Book/CD Pack $12.99

14. JOHNNY CASH
00702615 Book/Online Audio $15.99

15. COUNTRY CLASSICS
00702834 Book/CD Pack $12.99

16. STANDARDS
00702835 Book/CD Pack $12.99

17. POP STANDARDS
00702836 Book/CD Pack $12.99

18. IRISH SONGS
00703086 Book/Online Audio $12.99

19. BLUES STANDARDS
00703087 Book/CD Pack $12.99

20. FOLK POP ROCK
00703088 Book/CD Pack $12.99

21. HAWAIIAN CLASSICS
00703097 Book/CD Pack $12.99

22. ISLAND SONGS
00703098 Book/CD Pack $12.99

23. TAYLOR SWIFT
00221966 Book/Online Audio $16.99

24. WINTER WONDERLAND
00101871 Book/CD Pack $12.99

25. GREEN DAY
00110398 Book/CD Pack $14.99

26. BOB MARLEY
00110399 Book/Online Audio $14.99

27. TIN PAN ALLEY
00116358 Book/CD Pack $12.99

28. STEVIE WONDER
00116736 Book/CD Pack $14.99

29. OVER THE RAINBOW & OTHER FAVORITES
00117076 Book/Online Audio $15.99

30. ACOUSTIC SONGS
00122336 Book/CD Pack $14.99

31. JASON MRAZ
00124166 Book/CD Pack $14.99

32. TOP DOWNLOADS
00127507 Book/CD Pack $14.99

33. CLASSICAL THEMES
00127892 Book/Online Audio $14.99

34. CHRISTMAS HITS
00128602 Book/CD Pack $14.99

35. SONGS FOR BEGINNERS
00129009 Book/Online Audio $14.99

36. ELVIS PRESLEY HAWAII
00138199 Book/Online Audio $14.99

37. LATIN
00141191 Book/Online Audio $14.99

38. JAZZ
00141192 Book/Online Audio $14.99

39. GYPSY JAZZ
00146559 Book/Online Audio $15.99

40. TODAY'S HITS
00160845 Book/Online Audio $14.99

HAL•LEONARD®
www.halleonard.com

Prices, contents, and availability subject to change without notice.

The Best Songs Ever

70 songs have now been arranged for ukulele. Includes: Always • Bohemian Rhapsody • Memory • My Favorite Things • Over the Rainbow • Piano Man • What a Wonderful World • Yesterday • You Raise Me Up • and more.

00282413 . . . . $17.99

Campfire Songs for Ukulele

30 favorites to sing as you roast marshmallows and strum your uke around the campfire. Includes: God Bless the U.S.A. • Hallelujah • The House of the Rising Sun • I Walk the Line • Puff the Magic Dragon • Wagon Wheel • You Are My Sunshine • and more.

00129170 . . . . $14.99

The Daily Ukulele

arr. Liz and Jim Beloff
Strum a different song everyday with easy arrangements of 365 of your favorite songs in one big songbook! Includes favorites by the Beatles, Beach Boys, and Bob Dylan, folk songs, pop songs, kids' songs, Christmas carols, and Broadway and Hollywood tunes, all with a spiral binding for ease of use.

00240356 Original Edition $39.99
00240681 Leap Year Edition $39.99
00119270 Portable Edition $37.50

Disney Hits for Ukulele

Play 23 of your favorite Disney songs on your ukulele. Includes: The Bare Necessities • Cruella De Vil • Do You Want to Build a Snowman? • Kiss the Girl • Lava • Let It Go • Once upon a Dream • A Whole New World • and more.

00151250 . . . . $16.99

Also available:

00291547 **Disney Fun Songs for Ukulele** . . . $16.99
00701708 **Disney Songs for Ukulele** $14.99
00334696 **First 50 Disney Songs on Ukulele** . $16.99

First 50 Songs You Should Play on Ukulele

An amazing collec-tion of 50 accessible, must-know favorites: Edelweiss • Hey, Soul Sister • I Walk the Line • I'm Yours • Imagine • Over the Rainbow • Peaceful Easy Feeling • The Rainbow Connection • Riptide • more.

00149250 . . . . $16.99

Also available:

00292082 **First 50 Melodies on Ukulele** . . . $15.99
00289029 **First 50 Songs on Solo Ukulele** . . $15.99
00347437 **First 50 Songs to Strum on Uke** . $16.99

40 Most Streamed Songs for Ukulele

40 top hits that sound great on uke! Includes: Despacito • Feel It Still • Girls like You • Happier • Havana • High Hopes • The Middle • Perfect • 7 Rings • Shallow • Shape of You • Something Just like This • Stay • Sucker • Sunflower • Sweet but Psycho • Thank U, Next • There's Nothing Holdin' Me Back • Without Me • and more!

00298113 . . . . $17.99

The 4 Chord Songbook

With just 4 chords, you can play 50 hot songs on your ukulele! Songs include: Brown Eyed Girl • Do Wah Diddy Diddy • Hey Ya! • Ho Hey • Jessie's Girl • Let It Be • One Love • Stand by Me • Toes • With or Without You • and many more.

00142050 . . . . $16.99

Also available:

00141143 **The 3-Chord Songbook** $16.99

Pop Songs for Kids

30 easy pop favorites for kids to play on uke, including: Brave • Can't Stop the Feeling! • Feel It Still • Fight Song • Happy • Havana • House of Gold • How Far I'll Go • Let It Go • Remember Me (Ernesto de la Cruz) • Rewrite the Stars • Roar • Shake It Off • Story of My Life • What Makes You Beautiful • and more.

00284415 . . . . $16.99

Simple Songs for Ukulele

50 favorites for standard G-C-E-A ukulele tuning, including: All Along the Watchtower • Can't Help Falling in Love • Don't Worry, Be Happy • Ho Hey • I'm Yours • King of the Road • Sweet Home Alabama • You Are My Sunshine • and more.

00156815 . . . . $14.99

Also available:

00276644 **More Simple Songs for Ukulele** . $14.99

Top Hits of 2020

18 uke-friendly tunes of 2020 are featured in this collection of melody, lyric and chord arrangements in standard G-C-E-A tuning. Includes: Adore You (Harry Styles) • Before You Go (Lewis Capaldi) • Cardigan (Taylor Swift) • Daisies (Katy Perry) • I Dare You (Kelly Clarkson) • Level of Concern (twenty one pilots) • No Time to Die (Billie Eilish) • Rain on Me (Lady Gaga feat. Ariana Grande) • Say So (Doja Cat) • and more.

00355553 . . . . $14.99

Also available:

00302274 **Top Hits of 2019** $14.99

Ukulele: The Most Requested Songs

Strum & Sing Series
Cherry Lane Music
Nearly 50 favorites all expertly arranged for ukulele! Includes: Bubbly • Build Me Up, Buttercup • Cecilia • Georgia on My Mind • Kokomo • L-O-V-E • Your Body Is a Wonderland • and more.

02501453 . . . . $14.99

The Ultimate Ukulele Fake Book

Uke enthusiasts will love this giant, spiral-bound collection of over 400 songs for uke! Includes: Crazy • Dancing Queen • Downtown • Fields of Gold • Happy • Hey Jude • 7 Years • Summertime • Thinking Out Loud • Thriller • Wagon Wheel • and more.

00175500 9" x 12" Edition $45.00
00319997 5.5" x 8.5" Edition $39.99